KISAH SANG ANGKA

THE NUMBER STORY

SMALL BOOK ONE

ENGLISH - INDONESIAN

Numbers Teach Children
Their Number Names

written and illustrated by

MISS ANNA

Early Reader Edition of *The Number Story 1*
Bronze Medal Winner, 2016 Wishing Shelf Book Award

Library of Congress Control Number: 2018902040

Names: Miss Anna, author.
Title: Number story : numbers teach children their number names / Miss Anna.
Description: Portland, OR: Lumpy Publishing, 2018.
Identifiers: ISBN 978-1-945977-28-2| LCCN 2018902040
Summary: The pictures and rhymes present stories which introduce numbers 0-10.
Subjects: LCSH Numeration—English--Indonesian--Pictorial works--Juvenile literature. | BISAC JUVENILE NONFICTION /
Languages: English--Indonesian
Classification: LCC QA141.3 .M57 2018 | DDC 513—dc23

Publisher: Lumpy Publishing
Website: www.missannabooks.com
Email: missanna@missannabooks.com

Paperback: ISBN 978-1-945977-28-2
Printed in the U.S.A.   1 3 5 7 9 10 8 6 4 2

Ingin belajar kisah
nama angka kami?

It is very easy and a lot of fun!
Ini sangat mudah dan
sangat menyenangkan!

Say-along our little jingle
Ucapkan bersama, jingle kecil kita!

starting from Number One!
Kita akan mulai dari Angka Satu!

1
ONE   looks like my one finger.
SATU
terlihat seperti satu jariku.

ONE!
SATU!

2

TWO trails a tail.

DUA

jejak sebuah ekor.

A TAIL! SEBUAH EKOR!

3

THREE has bumps.

TIGA

memiliki benjolan.

Lihat bukit hijau!
BERGELOMBANG! BERLEKUK!

4

FOUR carries a sail.

EMPAT membawa sebuah layar.

A SAIL!
PERAHU
DENGAN LAYAR!

5

FIVE   is a racing track.

LIMA

lintasan balap.

VROOM
VRUUUM!

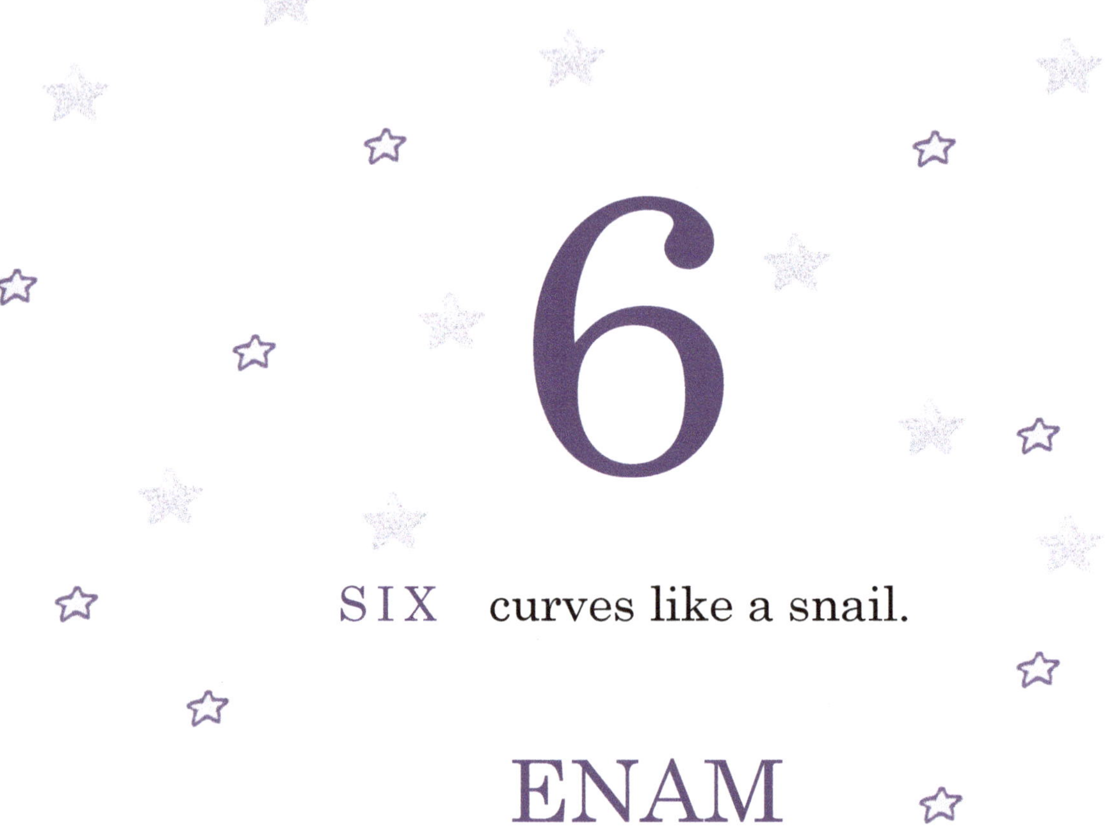

6

SIX   curves like a snail.

ENAM

berlekuk seperti siput.

A SNAIL! SEEKOR SIPUT!

7

SEVEN has a sharp angle.

TUJUH

punya sudut tajam.

OUCH!
ADUH!

8

EIGHT is rollercoaster rails.

DELAPAN

sebuah rel *rollercoaster*.

HURA!
YIPPEE!

NINE   is a bubble on a stick.

SEMBILAN

sebuah gelembung di atas tongkat.

A BUBBLE! SEBUAH GELEMBUNG!

10

TEN is an eye of a whale.

SEPULUH

satu mata ikan Paus.

WINK!
BERKEDIP!
HELLO! HALO!

And
Dan

0

ZERO   is an empty pail.

NOL

ember kosong.

IT'S EMPTY!
INI KOSONG!

Thank you for playing with us today.

We had a lot of fun too!

Terimakasih sudah bermain
bersama kami hari ini.
Kita juga bersenang senang!

We are your Number friends,
Zero to Ten,
Who will be here for you

Kita adalah teman-temanmu

Nol hingga Sepuluh.

Kita akan ada disini untuk kalian!

Bye-bye now!
See you again soon.

Selamat tinggal sekarang!

Sampai ketemu lagi!

The Numbers are *SINGING* too!

To sing-a-long, look for Miss Anna Number Story
at your favorite music store like iTUNES.

MP3

Numbers 0-10	Numbers 11-20	Numbers 0-100	About Clocks
IDENTIFYING & COUNTING	& Ordinals	& Place Values	& Telling Time
	first, second, third...	ones, tens, hundreds...	hours, minutes, seconds...

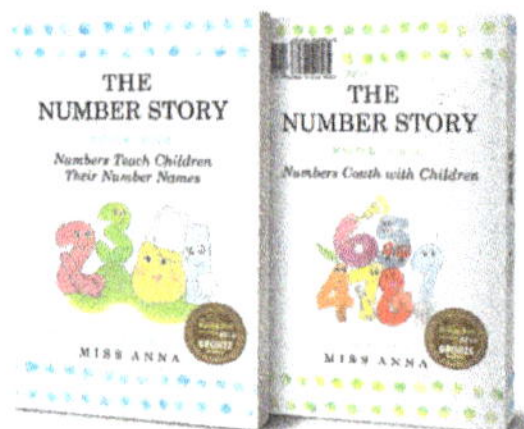

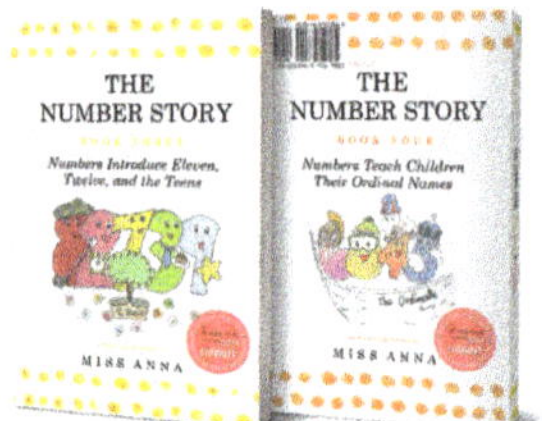

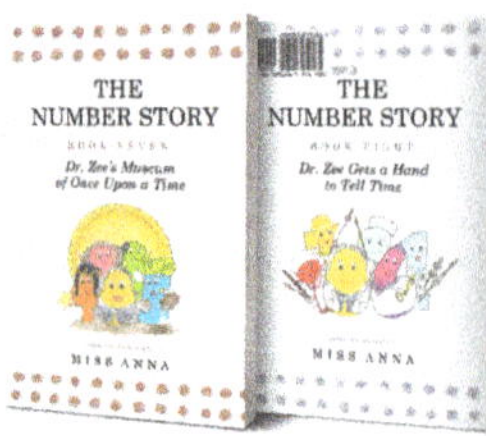

Number Story 1 & 2

isbn: 978-0-996216-48-7

Number Story 3 & 4

isbn: 978-1-945977-01-5

Number Story 5 & 6

isbn: 978-1-945977-06-0

Number Story 7 & 8

isbn: 978-1-949320-40-4

For more Miss Anna books to love,
visit us at

w w w . m i s s a n n a b o o k s . c o m

Numbers are working hard all over the world!
Come Travel the World with Us!